CW00801733

A LETTE
FRIENDS OF THE CROSS

Saint Louis de Montfort

CATHOLIC WAY
PUBLISHING

Copyright © 1950 by Montfort Publications, Bay Shore, L.I., N.Y. US.
Retypeset and republished in 2013 by Catholic Way Publishing.
Cover design by Catholic Way Publishing.

IMPRIMI POTEST:
S. Laurentii ad Separim die 3a Maii , 1950.
A. JOSSELIN, S.M.M.,
Superior General.

NIHIL OBSTAT:
MARTINUSJ. HEALY, S.T.D.,
Censor Librorum.

IMPRIMATUR:
± THOMAS EDMUNDUS MOLLOY, S.T.D.,
Episcopus Brooklyniensis.
Brooklynii, XX mensis Octobri s 1950.

Originally published in French by Saint Louis de Montfort as
"Lettre aux Amis de la Croix."

5" x 8" Paperback. Also available as an E-Book.
Kindle: ISBN-13: 978-1-78379-320-4
EPUB: ISBN-13: 978-1-78379-321-1

This work is published for the greater Glory of Jesus Christ through His most Holy Mother Mary and for the sanctification of the militant Church and her members.

10 9 8 7 6 5 4 3 2 1

ISBN-13: 978-1-78379-319-8

ISBN-10: 1-78379-319-8

CATHOLICWAYPUBLISHING.COM
LONDON, UK
2013

CONTENTS

»»»«««

PREFACE

〉〉〉》《《〈〈

St. Louis Mary De Montfort (1673–1716), author of this "Letter," is widely known through his treatise on "The True Devotion to the Blessed Virgin Mary" and its abridgment "The Secret of Mary." Well has he merited the title of "Apostle of Mary" and deservedly he is called "Tutor of the Legion of Mary." Addressing the many pilgrims at the canonization of St. De Montfort, July 1947, the Holy Father calls him "the guide who leads you to Mary and from Mary to Jesus." Speaking of St. Louis' "Prayer for Missionaries," Father Faber says:

"Since the Apostolical Epistles, it would be hard to find words that burn so marvelously." He has founded two religious congregations: the priests and the brothers of the Company of Mary (Montfort Fathers) and the Daughters of Wisdom. To his sons and daughters he has left a rich heritage of doctrinal writings.

In this "Letter" St. Louis manifests his passionate love for the Cross and pours forth the noble sentiments of his ardent soul. Like St. Paul, he is "determined to know nothing. . . . except Jesus Christ, and Him crucified" (1 Cor. 2–2); "indeed a stumbling block to the Jews and foolishness to the Gentiles, but to those who are called. . the Wisdom of God" (1 Cor 1–23, 24).

While giving missions in the city of Nantes in 1708, this eloquent preacher of the Cross and devout slave of Jesus in Mary formed, from the most fervent souls among his audiences, an association of "The Friends of the Cross." This fraternity or association was established .in the localities evangelized by the holy Missionary to fight against the many disorders and vices of the times and to make reparation for the outrages perpetrated against the Sacred Heart of Jesus. Each time he visited these places he exhorted the members to persevere in their first fervor. Alas! Suddenly he was forbidden to preach to them. Through intrigues, machinations and calumny his arch enemies, the Janseni sts, prevailed to have their redoubtable adversary si I enced.

During the summer of 1714 Father De Montfort stopped at Rennes. Here, too, with diabolical hate and fury, the Jansenists succeeded in having the saintly Missionary silenced. Welcoming this added humiliation—for his heaviest cross was to be without a cross—he took refuge at his al ma mater, the JEsui t College at Rennes, where he was warmly received. Here he buried himself in an eight day retreat meditating on the mystery of Calvary. From an incessant heart-to-heart talk with the Man of Sorrows and His Blessed Mother he received a new light and a more ardent love for the Crucified Savior.

On the last day of the retreat St. Louis, always eager to lead the faithful souls on the Royal Road of the Cross, desired to communicate to his fervent followers the fruits of his sublime meditation and poured forth the burning sentiments of his apostolic soul in the following "Letter."

In this epistle he gives us a holy doctrine which he preached and lived all his I if e thus imitating his Divine Master, Jesus Christ. It is believed that as a seminarian he wrote those two wonderful poems: "The Strength of Patience" (39 stanzas) and the "Triumph of the Cross" (31 stanzas) in which we find the elements contained in this "Letter." As a young priest he wrote his first book, "Love of Eternal Wisdom," and in its beautiful fourteenth chapter, "The Triumph of Eternal Wisdom in the Cross and by the Cross," is demonstrated the author's great love for the Folly of the Cross. In his allocution on St. De Montfort, quoted above, the Holy Father said: "Being crucified himself he has a perfect right to speak with authority on Christ Crucified. . . . He gives a sketch of his own life when drawing up a plan of life in his 'Letter to the Friends of the Cross' (Cf. "Letter," No. 4, *2)*.

When this "Letter" appeared St. Louis had already written the "Secret of Mary" and most probably had finished its lucid development "True Devotion to the Blessed Virgin Mary" to which this "Letter" is very closely related and is, as it were, the development and completion of the saintly author's "plan of forming a true client of Mary and a true disciple of Jesus Christ" (True Devotion No. 111).

Although written more than two centuries ago to fight against the evils and vices of those days this "Letter" retains all its usefulness and freshness. It wages a holy war on *the* evils, vices, pagan materialism and secularism of the present day. St. Louis gives us a panacea for all these ills: Christian mortification, prayer and a total consecration of ourselves to the Immaculate Heart of Mary. In a strong staccato tone he tells us "to suffer, to weep, to fast, to pray, to hide ourselves, to humiliate ourselves, to impoverish ourselves, to mortify ourselves. He who has not the spirit of Christ, which is the spirit of the Cross, does not belong to Him, but they who belong to Him have crucified their flesh and their concupiscence."

Is this not the message Our Lady of Fatima gave to the world— penance, mortification, sacrifice, prayer and consecration to her Immaculate Heart—in 1917. Is it not Our Blessed Mother who guided and inspired her faithful Apostle to write it!

Thus imbued with a burning love for Christ Crucified, a love born of humiliation, suffering, persecution and contempt, like his Divine Master, St. Louis gives us, at the close of his "Letter," some wise, prudent rules that teach us how to suffer and bear our crosses patiently, willingly and joyfully in the footsteps of Our Lord and Crucified Savior. Thus convinced of the necessity of the Cross, stimulated by the happy effects it produces in our souls, and guided by the same rules laid down by St. Louis De Montfort we will more readily renounce Satan, the world and the filth; we will more patiently bear our trials, crosses and tribulations and we will more carefully heed Christ's admonition: "If any one wishes to come after Me let him deny himself, and take up his cross daily and follow Me" (Luke: 8–23).

The Editor

INTRODUCTION

⧽⧽⧽⧸⧸⧸

Dear Friends of the Cross:

1. Since the divine Cross keeps me hidden and prevents me from speaking, I cannot, and do not even wish to express to you by word of mouth the feelings of my heart on the divine *excellence* and *practices* of your Association in the adorable Cross of Jesus Christ.

However, on this last day of my retreat, I come out, as it were, from the sweet retirement of my interior, to trace upon paper a few little arrows from the Cross with which to pierce your noble hearts. God grant that I could point them with the blood of my veins and not with the ink of my pen. Even if blood were required, mine, alas!, would be unworthy. May the spirit of the living God, then, be the life, vigor and tenor of this letter. May His unction be my ink, His divine Cross my pen and your hearts my paper.

PART I

EXCELLENCE OF THE ASSOCIATION OF THE FRIENDS OF THE CROSS

➤➤➤◄◄◄

I—GRANDEUR OF THE NAME, FRIENDS OF THE CROSS

2. Friends of the Cross, you are a group of crusaders united to fight against the world, not like those religious, men and women, who leave the world for fear of being overcome, but like brave, intrepid warriors on the battlefront, refusing to retreat or even to yield an inch. Be brave. Fight with all your might.

Bind yourselves together in that strong union of heart and mind which is far superior, far more terrifying to the world and hell! than the armed forces of a well-organized kingdom are to its enemies. Demons are united for your destruction, but you, be united for their overthrow; the avaricious are united to barter and hoard up gold and silver, combine your efforts in the pursuit of the eternal treasures hidden in the Cross; reprobates unite to make merry, but you, be united to suffer.

3. You call yourselves "Friends of the Cross." What a wonderful name! I must admit that it charms and fascinates me. It is brighter than the sun, higher than the heavens, more imposing and resplendent than any title given to king or emperor. It is the great name of Christ Himself, true God and true Man at one and the same time. It is the unmistakable title of a Christian.

4. Its splendor dazzles me but the weight of it frightens me. For this title implies that you have taken upon yourselves difficult and inescapable obligations, which are summed up in the words of the Holy Ghost: "A chosen generation, a kingly priesthood, a holy nation, a purchased people" (1 Peter *2*, 9).

A Friend of the Cross is one chosen by God from among ten thousand who have reason and sense for their only guide. He is truly divine, raised above reason and thoroughly opposed to the things of sense, for he lives in the light of true faith and burns with love for the Cross.

A Friend of the Cross is a mighty king, a hero who triumphs over the devil, the world and the flesh and their threefold concupiscence. He overthrows the pride of Satan by his love for humiliation, he triumphs over the world's geed by his love for poverty and he restrains the sensuality of the flesh by his love for suffering.

A Friend of the Cross is a holy man, separated from visible things. His heart is lifted high above al I that is frail and perishable; "his conversation is in heaven" (Phil. 3, 20); he journeys here below like a stranger and pilgrim. He keeps his heart free from the world, looks upon it with an unconcerned glance of his left eye and disdainfully tramples it under foot.

A Friend of the Cross is atrophy which the crucified Christ won on Calvary, in union with His Blessed Mother. He is another Benoni (Gen. 35, 18) or Benjamin, a son of sorrow, a son of the right hand. Conceived in the sorrowful heart of Christ, he comes into this world through the gash in the Savior's right side and is all empurpled in His blood. True to this heritage, he breathes forth only crosses and blood, death to the world, the flesh and sin and hides himself here below with Jesus Christ in God (Col. 3, 3).

Thus, a perfect Friend of the Cross is a true Christ-bearer, or rather another Christ, so much so that he can say with truth: "I live, now not I, but Christ liveth in me" (Gal. 2, 20).

5. My dear Friends of the Cross, does every act of yours justify what the eminent name you bear implies? Or at least are you, with the grace of God, in the shadow of Calvary's Cross and of Our Lady of Pity, really eager and truly striving to attain this goal? Is the way you follow the one that leads to this goal? Is it the true way of life, the narrow way, the thorn-strewn way to Calvary? Or are you unconsciously traveling the world's broad road, the road to perdition? Do you realize that there is a highroad which to all appearances is straight and safe for man to travel, but which in reality leads to death?

6. Do you really know the voice of God and grace from the voice of the world and human nature? Do you distinctly hear the

voice of God, our kind Father, pronouncing His three-fold curse upon everyone who follows the world in its concupiscence: "Woe, woe, woe to the inhabitants of the earth" (Apoc. 8, 13) and then appealing to you with outstretched arms: "Be separated, My chosen people (Is. 48,20; 52,11; Jer. 50,8; 51,6), beloved Friends of the Cross of My Son, be separated from those worldlings, for they are accursed by My Majesty, repudiated by My Son (John 17,9) and condemned by My Holy Spirit (John 16,8–12). Do not sit in their chair of pestilence; take no part in their gatherings; do not even step along their highways (Ps. 1,1). Hurry away from this great and infamous Babylon (Is. 48,20; Jer. 51,6); hearken only to the voice of My Beloved Son; follow only in His footprints; for He is the One I have given to be your Way, Truth, Life (John 14,6) and Model: hear ye Him" (Matt. 17,5; Luke 9,35; Mark 9,6; 2 Pet. 1,17).

Is your ear attentive to the pleadings of the lovable and cross-burdened Jesus, "Come, follow Me; he that followeth Me walketh not in darkness (John 8,12); have confidence, I have conquered the world" (John 16, 33)?

PART II

THE TWO GROUPS

⫸⫷

I—THE FOLLOWERS OF CHRIST AND THE FOLLOWERS OF THE WORLD

7. Dear Brethren, these are the two groups that appear before you each day, the followers of Christ and the followers of the world.

Our loving Savior's group is to the right, scaling a narrow path made all the narrower by the world's corruption. Our kind Master is *in* the lead, barefooted, thorn-crowned, robed in His blood and weighted with a heavy cross. There is only a handful of people who follow Him, but they are the bravest of the brave. His gentle voice is not heard above the tumult of the world, or men do not have the courage to follow Him in poverty, suffering, humiliation and in the other crosses His servants must bear all the days of their life.

II—THE OPPOSING SPIRIT OF THE GROUPS

8. To the left is the world's group, the devil's in fact, which is far superior in number, and seemingly far more colorful and splendid in array. Fashionable folk are all in a hurry to enlist, the highways are overcrowded, although they are broad and ever broadening with the crowds that flow through in a torrent. These roads are strewn with flowers, bordered with all kinds of amusements and attractions, and paved with gold and silver (Matt. 7,13–14).

9. To the right, the little flock that follows Jesus can speak only of tears, penance, prayer and contempt for worldly things Sobbing in their grief, they can be heard repeating: "Let suffer, let us weep, let us fast, let us pray, let us hide, let us humble ourselves, let us be

poor, let us mortify ourselves, for he who has not the spirit of Christ, the spirit of the Cross, is none of Christ's. Those who are Christ's have crucified their flesh with its concupiscence. We must be conformed to the image of Jesus Christ or else be damned!" "Be brave," they keep saying to each other, "be brave, for if God is for us, in us and leading us, who dare be against us? The One Who is dwelling within us is stronger than the one who is in the world; no servant is above his master; one moment of light tribulation worketh an eternal weight of glory; there are fewer elect than man may think; only the brave and daring take heaven by storm; the crown is given only to those who strive lawfully according to the Gospel, not according to the fashion of the world. Let us put all our strength into the fight, and run very fast to reach the goal and win the crown." Friends of the Cross spur each other on with such divine words.

10. Worldlings, on the contrary, rouse one another to persist in their unscrupulous depravity. "Enjoy life, peace and pleasure," they shout, "Enjoy life, peace and pleasure. Let us eat, let us drink, let us sing, let us dance, let us play. God is good, He did not make us to damn us; God does not forbid us to enjoy ourselves; we shall not be damned for that; away with scruples; we shall not die." And so they continue.

III—LOVING APPEAL OF JESUS

11. Dear Brethren, remember that our beloved Jesus has His eyes upon you at this moment, addressing you individually: "See how almost everybody leaves Me practically alone on the royal road of the Cross. Blind idol- worshipers sneer at My Cross and brand it folly. Obstinate Jews are scandalized at the sight of it as at some monstrosity (1 Cor. 1,23). Heretics tear it down and break it to pieces out of sheer contempt. But one thing I cannot say without My eyes filling with tears and My heart being pierced with grief is that the very children I nourished in My bosom and trained in My school, the very members I quickened with My spirit have turned against Me, forsaken Me and joined the ranks of the enemies of My Cross (Is. 1,2; Phil. 3,18). Would you also leave Me? (John 6,68). Would you also forsake me and flee from My Cross, like the world-lings, who are acting as so many Anti -Christs? (1 John 2,12). Would

you subscribe to the standards of the day (Rom. 12,2), despise the poverty of My Cross and go in quest of riches; shun the sufferings connected with My Cross, to run after pleasure; spurn the humiliations that must be borne with My Cross, and pursue worldly honors? There are many who pretend that they are friends of Mine and love M e but in reality they hate M e because they have no love for My Cross. I have many friends of My table, but few indeed of My Cross." (Imitation of Jesus Christ, Book 2, Chap. 11.)

12. In answer to the gracious invitation which Jesus extends, let us rise above ourselves. Let us not, like Eve, listen to the insidious suggestion of sense. Let us look up to the unique Author and Finisher of our faith, Jesus crucified (Heb. 12,2). Let us fly from the corrupting concupiscence and enticements of a corrupt world (2 Pet. 1,4). Let us love Jesus in the right way, standing by Him through the heaviest of crosses. Let us meditate seriously on these remarkable words of our beloved Master which sum up the Christian life in its perfection: "If any man will come after Ma let him deny hi mself, and take up his cross, and follow Me" (Matt. 16,24).

PART III

PRACTICES OF CHRISTIAN PERFECTION, THE DIVINE MASTER'S PROGRAM

❯❯❯❮❮❮

13. Christian perfection consists:

1. in willing to become a saint: "If any man will come after Me";

2. in self-denial . "Let him deny himself";

3. in suffering: "Let him take up his cross";

4. in doing: "Let him follow Me."

14. If *anyone,* not *many a one,* shows that the elect who are willing to be made conformable to the crucified Christ by carrying their cross are few in number. It would cause us to faint away from grief to learn how surprisingly small is their number.

It is so small that among ten thousand people there is scarcely one to be found, as was revealed to several Saints, among whom St. Simon Stylita, referred to by the holy Abbot Ni I us, followed by St. Basil, St. Ephrem and others. So small, indeed, that if God willed to gather them together, He would have to cry out as he did of yore through the voice of a prophet: "Come ye together one by one" (Is. 27,12), one from this province and one from that kingdom.

[*St. De Montfort here speaks of that small group of saintly souls who carry their cross more perfectly. He does not, however, exclude from salvation that vast multitude of less perfect Christians which the mercy of God wills to save.*]

15. If anyone *wills:* if a person has a real and definite determination and is prompted not by natural feelings, habit, self-love, personal interest or human respect but by an all-masterful grace of the Holy Ghost which is not communicated indiscriminately: "it is not given to all men to understand this mystery" (Matt. 13,11). In fact, only a privileged number of men receive this practical knowledge of the mystery of the Cross. For that man who climbs up to Calvary and lets himself be nailed on the Cross with Jesus in the heart of his own country must be a brave man, a hero, a resolute man, one who is lifted up in God, who treats as muck both the world and hell, as well as his very body and his own will. He must be resolved to relinquish all things, to undertake anything and to suffer everything for Jesus.

Understand this, dear Friends of the Cross, should there be anyone among you who has not this firm resolve, he is just limping along on one foot, flying with one wing, and undeserving of your company, since he is not worthy to be called a Friend of the Cross, for we must love the Cross as Jesus Christ loved it "with a great heart and a willing mind" (2 Mach. 1,3). That kind of half-hearted will is enough to spoil the whole flock, like a sheep with the scurvy. If any such one has slipped into your fold through the contaminated door of the world, then in the name of the crucified Christ, drive him out as you would a wolf from your sheepfold.

16. "If anyone will come *after Me*": for I have humbled Myself and reduced Myself to mere nothingness in such a way that I made Myself a worm rather than a man: "I am a worm and no man" (Ps. 21,7). *After Me:* for if I came into the world, it was only to espouse the Cross: "Behold I am come" (Ps. 39,8; Heb. 10,7–9); to set the cross in My heart of hearts: "In the midst of my heart" (Ps. 39,9); to love it from the days of my youth: "I have loved it from my youth" (Wisdom 8,2); only to long for it all the days of my life: "how straitened I am" (Luke 12,50); only to bear it with a joy I preferred even to the joys and delights that heaven and earth could offer: "Who, having joy set before him, endured the cross" (Heb. 12,2); and, finally, not to be satisfied until I had expired in its divine embrace.

II—SELF-DENIAL

17. Therefore, if anyone wants to come after Me, annihilated and crucified, he must glory as I did only in the poverty, humiliation and suffering of My Cross: "let him deny himself" (Matt. 16,24).

Far be from the Company of the Friends of the Cross those who pride themselves in suffering, the worldly-wise, elated geniuses and self-conceited individuals who are stubborn and puffed-up with their lights and talents Far be they from us, those endless talkers who make plenty of noise but bring forth no other fruit than vainglory.

Far from us those high-browed devotees everywhere displaying the self-sufficient pride of Lucifer: "I am not like the rest!" (Luke 18,11). Far be from us those who must always justify themselves when blamed, resist when attacked and exalt themselves when humbled.

Be careful not to admit into your fellowship those frail, sensitive persons who are afraid of the slightest pin-prick, who sob and sigh when faced with the lightest suffering, who have never experienced a hair-shirt, a discipline or any other penitential instrument, and who, with their fashionable devotions, mingle the most artful delicacy and the most refined lack of mortification.

III—SUFFERING

18. *Let him take up his cross,* the one that is *his.* Let this man or this woman, rarely to be found and worth more than the entire world (Prov. 31,10–31), take up with joy, fervently clasp in his arms and bravely set upon his shoulders this cross that is his own and not that of another; his own cross, the one that My Wisdom designed for him in every detail of number, weight and measurement; his own cross whose four dimensions, its length, breadth, thickness and height (Eph. 3,18), I very accurately gauged with My own hands; his own cross which all out of love for him I carved from a section of the very Cross I bore on Calvary; his cross, the grandest of all the gifts I have for My chosen ones on earth; his cross, made up in its thickness of temporal loss, humiliation, disdain, sorrow, illness and spiritual trial which My Providence will not fail to supply him with every day of his life; his cross, made up in its length of a definite

period of days or months when he will have to bear with slander or be helplessly stretched out on a bed of pain, or forced to beg, or else a prey to temptation, dryness, desolation and many another mental anguish; his cross, made up in its breadth of hard and bitter situations stirred up for him by his relatives, friends or servants; his cross, finally, made up in its depth of secret sufferings which I will have him endure nor will I allow him any comfort from created beings, for by My order they will turn from him too and even join Me in making him suffer.

19. Let him *carry* it, and not drag it, not shoulder it off, not lighten it, nor hide it. Let him hold it high in hand, without impatience or peevishness, without voluntary complaint or grumbling, without dividing or softening, without shame or human respect.

Let him place it on his forehead and say with St. Paul: "God forbid that I should glory save in the Cross of Our Lord Jesus Christ" (Gal. 6,14).

Let him carry it on his shoulders, after the example of Jesus Christ, and make it his weapon to victory and the scepter of his empire (Is 9,16).

Let him root it in his heart and there change it into a fiery bush, burning day and night with the pure love of God, without being consumed.

20. *The cross:* it is the *cross* he must carry for there is nothing more necessary, more useful, more agreeable and more glorious than suffering for Jesus Christ.

21. All of you are sinners and there is not a single one who is not deserving of hell; I myself deserve it the most. These sins of ours must be punished either here or hereafter. If they are punished in this world, they will not be punished in the world to come.

If we agree to God's punishing here below, this punishment will be dictated by love. For mercy, which holds sway in this world, will mete out the punishment, and not strict justice. This punishment will be light and momentary, blended with merit and sweetness and followed up with reward both in time and eternity.

22. But if the punishment due to our sins is held over for the next world, then God's avenging justice, which means fire and blood, will see to the punishing. What horrible punishment! How incomprehensible, how unspeakable! "Who knoweth the power of thy anger?" (Ps. 89,11). Punishment devoid of mercy (James 2,13),

pity, mitigation or merit; without limit and without end. Yes, without end! That mortal sin of a moment that you committed, that deliberate evil thought which now escapes your memory, the word that is gone with the wind, that act of such short duration against God's law—they shall all be punished for an eternity, punished with the devils of hell, as long as God is God! The God of vengeance will have no pity on your torments or your sobs and tears, violent enough to cleave the rocks. Suffering and still more suffering, without merit, without mercy and without end!

23. Do we think of this, my dear Brothers and Sisters, when we have some trial to undergo here below? Blessed indeed are we who have the privilege of exchanging an eternal and fruitless penalty for a temporary and meritorious suffering, just by patiently carrying our cross. What debts we still have to pay! How many sins we have committed which, despite a sincere confession and heartfelt contrition, will have to be atoned for in Purgatory for many a century, simply because in this world we were satisfied with a few insignificant penances! Let us settle our debts with good grace here below in cheerfully bearing our crosses, for in the world to come everything must be expiated, even the idle word (Matt. 12,36) and even to the last farthing. If we could lay hands on the devil's death-register in which he has noted down all our sins and the penalty to be paid, what a heavy debit we would find and how joyfully we would suffer many years here on earth rather than a single day in the world to come.

24. Do you not flatter yourselves, Friends of the Cross, that you are, or that you want to be, the friends of God? Be firmly resolved then to drink of the chalice which you must necessarily drink if you wish to enjoy the friendship of God. "They drank the chalice of the Lord and became the friends of God" (Common of Apostles, Lesson 7). The beloved Benjamin had the chalice while his brothers had only the wheat (Gen. 44,1–4). The disciple whom Jesus preferred had his Master's heart, went up with Him to Calvary and drank of the chalice. "Can you drink my chalice?" (Matt 20,22). To desire God's glory is good, indeed, but to desire it and pray for it without being resolved to suffer all things is mere folly and senseless asking. "You know not what you ask (Matt. 20,2 2) . . . you must undergo much suffering" (Acts 14,21): you must, it is necessary, it is indispensable!

We can enter the kingdom of heaven only at the price of many crosses and tribulations.

25. You take pride in being God's children and you do well; but you should also rejoice in the lashes your good Father has given you and in those He still means to give you; for He scourges every one of His children (Prov. 3,11; Heb. 13,5–6; Apoc. 3,19). If you are not of the household of His beloved sons, then—how unfortunate! what a calamity!—you are, as St. Augustine says, listed with the reprobate. Augustine also says: "The one that does not mourn like a stranger and wayfarer in this world cannot rejoice in the world to come as a citizen of heaven" (Sermon 31, 5 and 6). If God the Father does not send you worth-while crosses from time to time, that is because He no longer cares for you and is angry at you. He considers you a stranger, an outsider undeserving of His hospitality, or an unlawful child who has no right to share in his father's estate and no title to his father's supervision *and* discipline.

26. Friends of the Cross, disciples of a crucified God, the mystery of the Cross is a mystery unknown to the Gentiles, repudiated by the Jews and spurned by both heretics and bad Catholics, yet it is the great mystery which you must learn to practice at the school of Jesus Christ and which you can learn only at His School. You would look in vain for any philosopher who taught it in the Academies of ancient times; you would ask in vain either the senses or reason to throw any light on it, for Jesus alone, through His triumphant grace, is able to teach you this mystery and make you relish it.

Become proficient, therefore, in this super-eminent branch of learning under such a skillful Master. Having this knowledge, you will be possessed of all other branches of learning, for it surpassingly comprises them all. The Cross is our natural as well as our supernatural philosophy. It is our divine and mysterious theology. It is our philosopher-stone which, by dint of patience, is able to transmute the grossest of metals into precious ones, the sharpest pain into delight, poverty into wealth and the deepest humiliation into glory. He amongst you who knows how to carry his cross, though he know not A from B, towers above all others in learning.

Listen to the great St. Paul, after his return from the third heaven, where he was initiated into mysteries which even the Angels had not learned. He proclaims that he knows nothing and wants to know nothing but Jesus Christ crucified (1 Cor. 2,2). You can rejoice, then, if you happen to be a poor man without any schooling or a poor woman deprived of intellectual attainments, for if you know how to suffer with joy you are far more learned than a doctor of the Sorbonne who is unable to suffer as you do.

27. You are members of Jesus Christ (1 Cor. 6,15; 12,27; Eph. 5,30). What an honor! But, also, what need for suffering this entails! When the Head is crowned with thorns should the members be wearing a laurel of roses? When the Head is jeered at and covered with mud from Calvary's road should its members be enthroned and sprayed with perfume? When the Head has no pillow on which to rest, should its members be reclining on soft feathers? What an unheard of monster such a one would be! No, no, dear companions of the Cross, make no mistake. The Christians you see around you, fashionably attired, super-sensitive, excessively haughty and sedate, are neither true disciples nor true members of the crucified Jesus. To think otherwise would be an insult to your thorn-crowned Head and His Gospel truth.

My God! How many would-be Christians there are who imagine they are members of the Savior when in reality they are His most insidious persecutors, for while blessing themselves with the sign of the Cross, they crucify Him in their hearts

If you are led by the spirit of Jesus and are living the same life with Him, your thorn-crowned Head, then you must look forward to nothing but thorns, nails and lashes, in a word, to nothing but across.

A real disciple needs to be treated as his Master was, a member as its Head. And if the Head should offer you, as He offered St. Catherine of Siena, the choice between a crown of thorns and a crown of roses, do as she did and grasp the crown of thorns, fastening it tightly to your brow in the likeness of Jesus.

28. You are aware of the fact that you are living temples of the Holy Spirit (1 Cor. 6,19) and that, like living stones (1 Pa 2,5), you are to be placed by the God of love in the heavenly Jerusalem He is building. You must expect then to be shaped, cut and chiseled under the hammer of the Cross, otherwise you would remain unpolished stone, of no value at all, to be disregarded and cast aside. Do not cause the hammer to recoil when it strikes you. Yield to the chisel that is carving you and the hand that is shaping you. It may be that this skillful and loving Architect wants to make you a cornerstone in

His eternal edifice, one of His most faithful portraits in the heavenly kingdom. So let Him see to it. He loves you, He really loves you; He knows what He is doing, He has e experience. Love is behind every one of His telling strokes; nor will a single stroke miscarry unless your impatience deflects it.

29. At times the Holy Spirit compares the cross to a winnowing that clears the good grain from the chaff and dust (Matt. 3,13; Luke 3,17). Like grain in the winnowing, then, let yourself be shaken up and tossed about without resistance, for the Father of the household is winnowing you and will soon have you in His harvest. He also likens the cross to a fire whose intense heat burns rust off iron. God is a devouring fire (Deut. 4,24; 9,3; Heb. 13,29) dwelling in our souls through His Cross, purifying them yet not consuming them, exemplified in the past in a burning bush (Ex. 3,2–3). He likens it at times to the crucible of a forge where gold is refined (Prov. 17,3; Eccli. 2,5) and dross vanishes in smoke, but, in the processing, the precious metal must be tried by fire while the baser constituents go up in smoke and flame. So, too, in the crucible of tribulation and temptation, true Friends of the Cross are purified by their constancy in suffering while the enemies of the Cross vanish in smoke by their impatience and murmurings.

30. Behold, dear Friends of the Cross, before you a great cloud of witnesses (Heb. 12,1–2) who silently testify that what I assert is the truth. For instance, consider Abel, a righteous man, who was slain by his own brother; then Abraham, a righteous man, who journeyed on the earth like a wanderer; Lot, a righteous man, who was driven from his own country; Jacob, a righteous man, who was persecuted by his own brother; Tobias, a righteous man, who was stricken with blindness; Job, a righteous man, who was pauperized, humiliated and covered with sores from the crown of his head to the sol cm of his feet.

31. Consider the countless Apostles and Martyrs who were bathed in their own blood; the countless Virgins and Confessors who were pauperized, humiliated, exiled and cast aside. Like St. Paul they fervently proclaim: Behold our beloved Jesus, "Author and Finisher of the faith" (Heb. 12,2) we put in Him and in His Cross; it was necessary for Him to suffer and so to enter through the Cross into His glory (Luke 24,26).

There at the side of Jesus consider Mary, who had never known either original or actual sin, yet whose tender, Immaculate Heart was pierced with a sharp sword even to its very depths. If I had time to dwell on the Passion of Jesus and Mary, I could prove that our sufferings are naught compared to theirs.

32. Who, then, would dare claim exemption from the cross? Who would refuse to rush to the very place where he knows he will find a cross awaiting him? Who would refuse to borrow the words of the martyr, St. Ignatius: "Let fire and gallows, wild beasts and all the torments of the devil assail me, so that I may rejoice in the possession of Jesus Christ."

33. If you have not the patience to suffer and the generosity to bear your cross like the chosen ones of God, then you will have to trudge under its weight, grumbling and fretting like reprobates; like the two animals that dragged the Ark of the Covenant, lowing as they went (1 Kings 6,12); like Simon the Cyrenaean who unwillingly put his hand to the very Cross of Christ (Matt. 27,32; Mark 15,21), complaining while he carried it. You will be like the impenitent thief who from the summit of his cross plunged headlong into the depths of the abyss.

No, the cursed earth on which we live cannot give us happiness. We can see none too clearly in this benighted land. We are never perfectly calm on this troubled sea. . We are never without warfare in a world of temptation and battlefields We cannot escape scratches on a thorn-covered earth. Both elect and reprobate must bear their cross here, either willingly or unwillingly. Remember these words:

"Three crosses stand on Calvary's height
One must be chosen, so choose aright;
Like a saint you must suffer, or a penitent thief,
Or like a reprobate, in endless grief."

This means that if you will not suffer gladly as Jesus did, or patiently like the penitent thief, then you must suffer despite yourself like the impenitent thief. You will have to drain the bitterest chalice even to the dregs, and with no hope of relief through grace.

You will have to bear the entire weight of your cross, and without the powerful help of Jesus Christ. Then, too, you will have that awful weight to bear which the devil will add to your cross, by means of the impatience the cross will cause you. After sharing the impenitent thief's unhappiness here on earth, you will meet him again in the fires of hell.

34. But if you suffer as you should, your cross will be a sweet yoke (Matt. 11,30), for Christ will share it with you. Your soul will be borne on it as on a pair of wings to the portals of Heaven. It will be the mast on your ship guiding you happily and easily to the harbor of salvation.

Carry your cross with patience: across patiently borne wi II be your light in spiritual darkness, for he knows naught who knows not how to suffer (Eccli. 34,9).

Carry your cross with joy and you will be inflamed with divine love, for only in suffering can we dwell in the pure love of Christ.

Roses are only gathered from among thorns. As wood is fuel for the fire, so too is the Cross the only fuel for God's love. Remember that saying we read in the "Following of Christ": "Inasmuch as you do violence to yourself," suffering patiently, "insofar do you advance" in divine love (Bk. 1, Chap. 15,11). Do not expect anything great from those fastidious, slothful souls who refuse the Cross when it approaches and who do not go in search of any, when discretion allows. What are they but unti I led soil, which can produce only thorns because it has not been turned up, harrowed and furrowed by a judicious laborer. They are like stagnant water which is unfit for ether washing or drinking.

Carry your cross joyfully and none of your enemies will be able to resist its conquering strength (Luke 21,15), while you yourself will enjoy its relish beyond compare. Yes, indeed, Brethren, remember that the real Paradise here on earth is to be found in suffering for Jesus, Ask the saints. They will tell you that they never tasted a banquet so delicious to the soul than when undergoing the severest torments. St. Ignatius the Martyr said: "Let all the torments of the devil come upon me!" "Either suffering or death!," said St. Theresa, and St. Magdalen de Pazzi: "Not death but suffering!" "May I suffer and be despised for Thy sake," said Blessed John of the Cross. In reading the lives of the saints we find many others speaking in the self-same terms.

Dear Brethren, believe the Word of God, for the Holy Spirit says: The Cross affords all kinds of joy to anyone without exception who suffers cheerfully for God, (Jas. 1,2). The joy that springs from the cross is keener than the joy which a poor person would experience if over-laden with an abundance of riches, than the joy of a peasant who is made ruler of his country, than the joy of a commander-in-chief over the victories he has won, than the joy of a prisoner released from his fetters. In conclusion, let us picture the greatest joys to be found here below: the joy of a crucified person who knows how to suffer not only equals them but even surpasses them all.

35. Be glad, therefore, and rejoice when God favors you with one of His choicest crosses, for without realizing it you are being blessed with the greatest gift that Heaven has, the greatest gift of God. Yes, the cross is God's greatest gift. If you could only understand this, you would have Masses said, you would make novenas at the tombs of the saints; you would undertake long pilgrimages, as did the saints, to obtain this divine gift from Heaven.

36. The world claims it is madness on your part, degrading and stupid, rash and reckless. Let the world, in its blindness, say what it likes. This blindness which is responsible for a merely human and distorted view of the cross is a source of glory for us. For every ti me they provide us with crosses by mocking and persecuting us, they are simply offering us jewels, setting us upon a throne and crowning us with laurels

37. What I say is but little. Take all the wealth and honors and scepters and brilliant diadems of monarchs and princes, says St. John Chrysostom, they are all insignificant compared with the glory of the Cross; it is greater even than the glory of the Apostles and the Sacred Writers. Enlightened by the Holy Spirit, this saintly man goes as far as to say: "If I were given the preference, I would gladly leave Heaven to suffer for the God of Heaven. I would prefer the darkness of a dungeon to the thrones of the highest heaven and the heaviest of crosses to the glory of the Seraphim.

Suffering for me is of greater value than the gift of miracles, the power to command the infernal spirits, to master the physical universe, to stop the sun in its course and to raise the dead to life. Per and Paul are more glorious in the shackles of a dungeon than in being lifted to the third heaven and presented with the keys to Paradise."

38. In fact, was it not the Cross that gave Jesus Christ "a name which is above all names; that in the name of Jesus every knee should bow of those that are in heaven, on earth and under the

earth" (Phil. 2,9–10). The glory of the one who knows how to suffer is so great that the radiance of his splendor rejoices heaven, angels and men and even the God of Heaven. If the saints in Heaven could still wish for something they would want to return to earth so as to have the privi le of bearing a cross.

39. If the cross is covered with such glory on earth, how magnificent it must be in Heaven. Who could ever understand and tell the eternal weight of glory we are given when, even for a single instant, we bear a cross as a cross should be borne (2 Cor. 4,17). Who could ever collate the glory that will be given in Heaven for the crosses and sufferings we carried for a year, perhaps even for a lifetime.

40. Evidently, my dear Friends of the Cross, heaven is preparing something grand for you, as you are told by a great Saint, since the Holy Ghost has united you so intimately to an object which the whole world so carefully avoids. Evidently, God wishes to make of you as many saints as you are Friends of the Cross, if you are faithful to your calling and dutifully carry your cross as Jesus Christ has carried His.

IV—IN CHRIST-LIKE FASHION

41. But mere suffering is not enough. For even the devil and the world have their martyrs. We must suffer and bear our crosses in the footsteps of Jesus. *Let him follow Me:* this means that we must bear our crosses as Jesus bore His. To help you do this, I suggest the following rules:

PART IV

FOURTEEN RULES TO FOLLOW
IN CARRYING ONE'S CROSS

≫≫≪≪

42. First. Do not, deliberately and through your own fault, procure crosses for yourself. You must not do evil in order to bring about good. You should never try to bring discredit upon yourself by doing things improperly, unless you have a special inspiration from on high. Strive rather to imitate Jesus Christ, who did all things well (Mark 7,37), not out of self-love or vainglory, but to please God and to win over His fellow-men. Even though you do the best you can in the performance of your duty, you will still have to contend with contradiction, persecution and contempt which Divine Providence will send you against your will and without your choice.

43. Second. Should your neighbor be scandalized, although without reason, at any action of yours which in itself is neither good nor bad, then, for the sake of charity, refrain from it, to avoid the scandal of the weak. This heroic act of charity will be of much greater worth than the thing you were doing or intended to do.

If, however, you are doing some beneficial or necessary thing for others and were unreasonably disapproved by a hypocrite or prejudiced person, then refer the matter to a prudent adviser, letting him judge of its expedience and necessity. Should his decision be favorable, you have only to continue and let these others talk, provided they take no means to prevent you. Under such circumstances, you have Our Lord's answer to His disciples when they informed Him that Scribes and Pharisees were scandalized at His words and deeds: "Let them alone; they are blind." (Matt. 15,14).

44. Third. Certain holy and distinguished persons have been asking for and seeking, or even, by eccentricities, bringing upon them-

selves, crosses, disdain and humiliation. Let us simply adore and
admire the extraordinary workings of the Holy Spirit in these souls.
Let us humble ourselves in the presence of this sublime virtue,
without making any attempt to reach such heights, for compared
with these racing eagles and roaring lions we are simply fledglings
and cubs

45. Fourth. You can nevertheless and even should ask for the
wisdom of the Cross, that sapid, experimental knowledge of the
truth, which, in the light of faith, shows us the deepest mysteries,
among others the mystery of the Cross. But this can be had only by
dint of hard toil, profound humiliation and fervent prayer. If you
need that perfect spirit (Ps. 50,14) which enables us to bear the
heaviest crosses with courage—that sweet, kindly spirit (Luke 11,13)
which enables us to relish in the higher part of the soul things that
are bitter and repulsive—that wholesome, upright spirit (Ps 50,12)
which seeks God and God alone—that all-embracing knowledge of
the Cross—briefly that infinite treasure which gives the soul that
knows how to make good use of it a share in the friendship of God
(Wisdom 7,14), ask for this wisdom, ask for it constantly, fervently,
without hesitation or fear of not obtaining it. You will certainly
obtain it and then see clearly, in the light of your own experience,
how it is possible to desire, seek and relish the Cross.

46. Fifth. If, inadvertently, you blunder into a cross, or even if
you do so through your own fault, forthwith humble yourselves
interiorly under the mighty hand of God (1 P. 5,6), but do not worry
over it. You might say to yourself: "Lord, there is another trick of
my trade." If the mistake you made was sinful, accept the humiliation you suffer as punishment. But if it was not sinful, then humbly
accept it in expiation of your pride. Often, actually very often, God
allows His greatest servants, those who are far advanced in grace, to
make the most humiliating mistakes. This humbles them in their
own eyes and in the eyes of their fellow men. It prevents them from
seeing and taking pride in the graces God bestows on them or in the
good deeds they do, so that, as the Holy Ghost declares: "no flesh
should glory in the sight of God" (1 Cor. 1,29).

47. Sixth. Be fully persuaded that through the sin of Adam and
through our own actual sins everything within ourselves is vitiated,
not only the senses of the body but even the powers of the soul. So
much so that as soon as the mind, thus vitiated, takes delight in

poring over some gift received from God, then the gift itself, or the
act or the grace is tarnished and vitiated and God no longer favors it
with His divine regard. Since looks and thoughts of the human mind
can spoil man's best actions and God's choicest gifts, what about
the acts which proceed from man's own will and which are more
corrupt than the acts of the mind?

So we need not wonder, when God hides His own within the
shadow of His countenance (Ps. 30,21), that they may not be defiled
by the regards of their fellow men or by their own self-
consciousness. What does not this jealous God allow and do to keep
them hidden! How often He humiliates them! Into how many faults
He permits them to fall! How often He allows them to be tempted
as St. Paul was tempted (2 Cor. 12,7)! In what a state of uncertainty,
perplexity and darkness He leaves them! How wonderful God is in
His saints, and in the means He takes to lead them to humility and
holiness!

48. Seventh. Be careful not to imitate proud self-centred zealots.
Do not think that your crosses are tremendous, that they are tests of
your fidelity to God and tokens of God's extraordinary love for you.
This gesture has its source in spiritual pride. It is a snare quite subtle
and beguiling but full of venom. You ought to acknowledge, first,
that you are so proud and sensitive that you magnify straws into
rafters, scratches into deep wounds, rats into elephants, a meaning-
less word, a mere nothing, in truth, into an outrageous, treasonable
insult. Second, you should acknowledge that the crosses God sends
you are really and truly loving punishments for your sins, and not
special marks of God's benevolence. Third, you must admit that He
is infinitely lenient when He sends you some cross or humiliation, in
comparison with the number and atrocity of your sins. For these
sins should be considered in the light of the holiness of a God
Whom you have offended and Who can tolerate nothing that is
defiled; in the light of a God dying and weighted down with sorrow
at the sight of your sins; in the light of an everlasting hell which you
have deserved a thousand times, perhaps a hundred thousand times.
Fourth, you should admit that the patience you put into suffering is
more tinged *than* you think with natural human motives. You have
only to note your little self-indulgences, your skillful seeking for
sympathy, these confidences you so naturally make to friends or
perhaps to your spiritual director, your quick, clever excuses, the

murmurings or rather the detractions so neatly worded, so charitably
spoken against those who have injured you, the exquisite delight you
take in dwelling on your misfortunes and that belief so characteristic
of Lucifer, that you are somebody (Acts 8,9), and so forth. Why I
should never finish if I were to point out all the ways and by-ways
human nature takes, even in its sufferings.

49. Eighth. Take advantage of your sufferings and more so of
the small ones than of the great. God considers not so much what
we suffer as how we suffer. To suffer much, yet badly, is to suffer
like reprobates. To suffer much, even bravely, but for a wicked
cause, is to suffer as a martyr of the devil. To suffer much or little
for the sake of God is to suffer like saints.

If it be right to say that we can choose our crosses, this is particularly true of the little and obscure ones as compared with the
huge, conspicuous ones, for proud human nature would likely ask
and seek for the huge, conspicuous crosses even to the point of
preferring them and embracing them. But to choose small, unno-
ticeable crosses and to carry them cheerfully requires the power of a
special grace and unshakeable fidelity to God. Do then as the store-
keeper does with his merchandise: make a profit on every article;
suffer not the loss of the tiniest fragment of the true Cross. It may
be only the sting of a fly or the point of a pin that annoys you, it
may be the little eccentricities of a neighbor, some unintentional
slight, the insignificant loss of a penny, some little restlessness of
soul, a slight physical weakness, a light pain in your limbs. Make a
profit on every article as the grocer does, and you will soon become
wealthy in God, as the grocer does in money, by adding penny to
penny in his till. When you meet with the least contradiction, simply
say: "Blessed be God! My God I thank you." Then treasure up in
the till of God's memory the cross which has just given you a profit.
Think no more of it, except to say: "Many thanks!" or, "Be merci-
ful!"

50. Ninth. The love you are told to have for the Cross is not
sensible love, for this would be impossible to human nature.

It is important to note the three kinds of love: sensible love, rational love and love that is faithful 'and supreme; in other words, the
love that springs from the lower part of man, the flesh; the love that
springs from the superior or part, his reason; and the love that

springs from the supreme part of man, from the summit of his soul, which is the intellect enlightened by faith.

51. God does not ask you to love the Cross with the will of the flesh. Since the flesh is the subject of evil and corruption, all that proceeds from it is evil and it cannot, of itself, submit to the will of God and His crucifying law. It was this aspect of His human nature which Our Lord referred to when He cried out, in the Garden of Olives: "Father, . . . not My will but Thine be done." (Luke 22,42). If the lower powers of Our Lord's human nature, though holy, could not love the Cross without interruption, then, with still greater reason, will our human nature, which is very much vitiated, repel it. At times, like many of the saints, we too may experience a feeling of even sensible joy in our sufferings, but that joy does not come from the flesh though it is in the flesh. It flows from our superior powers, so completely filled with the divine joy of the Holy Ghost, that it spreads to our lower powers. Thus a person who is undergoing the most unbearable torture is able to say: "My heart and my flesh have rejoiced in the living God" (Ps. 83,3).

52. There is another love for the Cross which I call rational, since it springs from the higher part of man, his reason. This love is wholly spiritual. Since it arises from the knowledge of the happiness there is in suffering for God, it can be and really is perceived by the soul. It also gives the soul inward strength and joy. Though this rational and perceptible joy is beneficial, even very beneficial, it is not an indispensable part of joyous, divine suffering.

53. This is why there is another love, which the masters of the spiritual life call the love of the summit and highest point of the soul and which the philosophers call the love of the intellect. When we possess this love, even though we experience no sensible joy or rational pleasure, we love and relish, in the light of pure faith, the cross we must bear, even though the lower part of our nature may often be in a state of warfare and alarm and may moan and groan, weep and sigh for relief; and thus we repeat with Jesus Christ: "Father . . . not My will but Thine be done" (Luke 22,42), or with the Blessed Virgin: "Behold the handmaid of the Lord, be it done to me according to Thy word" (Luke 1,38).

It is with one of these two higher loves that we should accept and love our cross.

54. Tenth. Be resolved then, dear Friends of the Cross, to suffer every kind of cross without excepting or choosing any: all poverty, all injustice, all temporal loss, all illness, all humiliation, all contradiction, all calumny, all spiritual dryness, all desolation, all interior and exterior trials. Keep saying: "My heart is ready, 0 God, my heart is ready" (Ps. 56,8). Be ready to be forsaken by men and angels and, seemingly, by God Himself. Be ready to be persecuted; envied, betrayed, calumniated, discredited and forsaken by everyone. Be ready to undergo hunger, thirst, poverty, nakedness, exile, imprisonment, the gallows and all kinds of torture, even though you are innocent of everything with which you may be charged. What if you were cast out of your own home like Job and Saint Elizabeth of Hungary; thrown, like this saint, into the mire; or dragged upon a manure pile like Job, malodorous and covered with ulcers, without anyone to bandage your wounds, without a morsel of bread, never refused to a horse or a dog? Add to these dreadful misfortunes all the temptations with which God allows the devil to prey upon you, without pouring into your soul the least feeding of consolation.

Firmly believe that this is the summit of divine glory and real happiness for a true, perfect Friend of the Cross.

55. Eleven. For proper suffering, form the pious habit of considering four things:

First, the Eye of God. God is like a great king, who from the height of a tower observes with satisfaction his soldier in the midst of the battle and praises his valor. What is it on earth that attracts God's attention? Kings and emperors on their thrones? He often looks at them with nothing but contempt. Brilliant victories of a nation's armies, precious stones, any such things that are great in the sight of men? "What is great to men is an abomination before God" (Luke 16,15). What then does God look upon with pleasure and delight? What is He asking the Angels about, and even the devils? It is about the man who is fighting for Him against riches, against the world, hell and himself, the man who is cheerfully carrying his cross. Hast thou not seen upon earth that great wonder which the heavens consider with admiration? said the Lord to Satan; "hast thou considered My servant Job" (Job 2,3) who is suffering for Me?

56. Second, the Hand of God, Every disorder in nature, from the greatest to the smallest, is the work of His almighty Hand. The Hand that devastates an army of a hundred thousand (2 Kings

19,35) will make a leaf drop from a tree and a hair fall from your head (Luke 2 1,18). The Hand that was laid so heavily upon Job is particularly light when it touches you with some little trial. This Hand fashions day and night, sun and darkness, good and evil. God permits the sin which provokes you; He is not the cause of its malice, although He does allow the act.

If anyone, then, treats you as Semei treated King David (2 Kings 16,5–11), loading you with insults and casting stones at you, say to yourself: "I must not mind; I must not take revenge for this is an ordinance of God. I know that I have deserved every abuse and it is only right that God punish me. Desist, my hands, and strike not; desist, my tongue, and speak not; the person who injures me by word or deed is an ambassador, mercifully sent by God to punish me as His love alone knows how. Let us not incur His justice by assuming His right to vengeance. Let us not despise His mercy by resisting the affectionate strokes of His lash, lest, for His vengeance, He should remand us to the rigorous justice of eternity."

Consider how God bears you up with one Hand, of infinite power and wisdom, while with the other He chastises you. With the one He deals out death, while with the other He dispenses life. He humbles you and raises you up. With both arms, He reaches sweetly and mightily (Wisdom 8,1) from the beginning of your life to its end. Sweetly: by not allowing you to be tempted or afflicted beyond your strength. Mightily: by favoring you with a powerful grace, proportioned to the vehemence and duration of your temptation or affliction. Mightily:—and the spirit of His holy Church bears witness—"He is your stay on the brink of a precipice, your guide along a misleading road, your shade in the scorching heat, your raiment in the pouring rain or the biting cold. He is your conveyance when you are utterly exhausted, your help in adversity, your staff on the slippery way. He is your port of refuge when, in the throes of a tempest, you are threatened with ruin and shipwreck."

57. Third, consider the Wounds and Sorrows of our crucified Jesus. Hear what He Himself has to say: "All ye that pass along the thorny and crucifying way I had to follow, look and see. Look with the eyes of your body; look with the eye of contemplation, and see if your poverty, nakedness, disgrace, sorrow, desolation are like unto Mine. Behold Ma innocent as I am, then will you complain, you who are guilty" (Lam. 1,12).

The Holy Ghost td Is us, by the mouth of the Apostles, that we should keep our eyes on Jesus Crucified (Gal. 3,1) and arm ourselves with this thought of Him (1 Pet. 4,1) which is our most powerful and most penetrating weapon against all our enemies. When you are assailed by poverty, disrepute, sorrow, temptation or any other cross, arm yourselves with this shield, this breastplate, this helmet, this two-edged sword (Eph. 6,12–18), that is, with the thought of Jesus crucified. There is the solution to your every problem, the means you have to vanquish all your enemies.

58. Fourth, lift up your eyes, behold the beautiful crown that awaits you in Heaven if you carry your cross as you should. That was the reward which kept patriarchs and prophets strong in faith under persecution. It gave heart to the Apostles and martyrs in their labors and torments. Patriarchs used to say as Moses had said: "We would rather be afflicted with the people of God," so as to enjoy eternal happiness with Him, "than to have the pleasure of sin for a short time (Heb. 11,25–26). The prophets repeated David's words: "We suffer great persecutions on account of the reward" (Ps. 63,8; 118,112). The Apostles and martyrs voiced the sentiments of St. Paul: "We are, as it were, men appointed to death: we are made a spectacle to the world, and to angels, and to men," by our sufferings "being made the offscouring of the world," (1 Cor. 4,9–13), "by reason of the exceeding and eternal weight of glory, which this momentary *and* light tribulation worketh in us" (2 Cor. 4,17).

Let us see and listen to the angels right above us: "Be careful not to forfeit the crown that is set aside for you if you bravely bear the cross that is given you. If you do not bear it well, someone will bear it in your stead and will take your crown. All the saints warn us: fight courageously, suffer patiently and you will be given an everlasting kingdom." Let us hear Jesus: "To him only will I give My reward who shall suffer and overcome through patience" (Apoc. 2,6; 11,17; 3,5; 21,7).

Let us lower our eyes and seethe place we deserve, the place that awaits us in hell in the company of the wicked thief and the reprobate, if we go through suffering as they did, resentful and bent on revenge. Let us exclaim after St. Augustine; "Burn. 0 Lord, cut, carve, divide in this world, in punishment for my sins, provided Thou pardon them in eternity."

59. Twelfth. Never murmur or deliberately complain about any created thing that God may use to afflict you. It is important to note the three kinds of complaints that may arise when misfortune assails you. The first is natural and involuntary. This happens when the human body moans and groans, sobs and sighs and weeps. If, as I said, the higher point of the soul submits to the will of God, there is no sin. The second is rational. Such is the case when we complain and disclose our hardship to some superior or physician who is able to remedy it. This complaint may be an imperfection, if too eagerly made, but it is no sin. The third is sinful. This happens when a person complains of others either to rid himself of the suffering they cause him, or to take revenge. Or else when he wilfully complains about the sorrow he must bear and shows signs of grief and impatience.

60. Thirteenth. Whenever you are given a cross, be sure to embrace it with humility and gratitude. If God, in His infinite goodness, favors you with a cross of some importance, be sure to thank him in a special way and have others join you in thanking him. Do as that poor woman did who, through an unjust lawsuit, lost everything she owned. She immediately offered the last few pennies she had, to have a Mass said in thanksgiving to Almighty God for the good fortune that had come to her.

61. Fourteenth. If you wish to be worthy of the Nisi crosses, those that are not of your choice, then, with the help of a prudent director, take on some that are voluntary.

Suppose you have a piece of furniture that you do not need but prize. Give it to some poor person, and say to yourself: "Why should I have things I do not need, when Jesus is destitute?"

Do you dislike certain kinds of food, the practice of some particular virtue, or some offensive odor? Taste this food, practice this virtue, endure this odor, conquer yourself.

Is your affection for some person or thing too ardent and tender? Keep away, deprive yourself, break away from things that appeal to you.

Have you that natural tendency to see and be seen, to be doing things or going someplace? Mind your eyes and hold your tongue, stop right where you are and keep to yourself.

Do you fed a natural aversion to some person or thing? Rise above self by keeping near them.

62. If you are truly Friends of the Cross, then, without your knowing it, love, which is always ingenious, will discover thousands of little crosses to enrich you. Then you need not fear self-conceit which often accompanies the patient endurance of conspicuous crosses and since you have been faithful in a few things, the Lord will keep His promise and set you over many things (Matt. *25,21,23)*: over many graces He will grant you; over many crosses He will send you; over much glory He will prepare for you

CATHOLIC WAY PUBLISHING
PAPERBACKS AND E-BOOKS

⇥⇥⇥⇤⇤⇤

True Devotion to Mary: With Preparation for Total Consecration
by Saint Louis De Montfort
> 5" x 8" Paperback: ISBN–13: 978-1-78379-000-5
> 6" x 9" Hardback: ISBN–13: 978-1-78379-004-3
> Kindle E-Book: ISBN–13: 978-1-78379-001-2
> EPUB E-Book: ISBN–13: 978-1-78379-002-9

The Secret of the Rosary by Saint Louis de Montfort
> 5" x 8" Paperback: ISBN–13: 978-1-78379-310-5
> Kindle E-Book: ISBN–13: 978-1-78379-311-2
> EPUB E-Book: ISBN–13: 978-1-78379-312-9

The Mystical City of God by Venerable Mary of Agreda
Popular Abridgement
> 5" x 8" Paperback: ISBN–13: 978-1-78379-063-0
> Kindle E-Book: ISBN–13: 978-1-78379-064-7
> EPUB E-Book: ISBN–13: 978-1-78379-065-4

The Imitation of Christ by Thomas a Kempis
> 5" x 8" Paperback: ISBN–13: 978-1-78379-037-1
> Kindle E-Book: ISBN–13: 978-1-78379-038-8
> EPUB E-Book: ISBN–13: 978-1-78379-039-5

My Daily Prayers by Catholic Way Publishing
> 5" x 8" Paperback: ISBN–13: 978-1-78379-027-2
> Kindle E-Book: ISBN–13: 978-1-78379-028-9
> EPUB E-Book: ISBN–13: 978-1-78379-029-6

The Three Ages of the Interior Life: Prelude of Eternal Life
by Reverend Reginald Garrigou-Lagrange O.P.
Volume One
> 5" x 8" Paperback: ISBN–13: 978-1-78379-296-2
> Kindle E-Book: ISBN–13: 978-1-78379-297-9
> EPUB E-Book: ISBN–13: 978-1-78379-298-6

Volume Two
> 5" x 8" Paperback: ISBN–13: 978-1-78379-299-3
> Kindle E-Book: ISBN–13: 978-1-78379-300-6
> EPUB E-Book: ISBN–13: 978-1-78379-301-3

WWW.CATHOLICWAYPUBLISHING.COM
LONDON, UK
2013

Made in the USA
Charleston, SC
12 February 2014